birth pangs

t.n. nelson

"Mule" previously published in *From Roots to Branches*. "Double Sorrowed," "The Harp and the Camera," and "No Second Cross" previously published in *Antiphon*.

Resource *Publications*
An imprint of *Wipf and Stock Publishers*
199 West 8th Avenue • Eugene OR 97401

Resource Publications
An imprint of Wipf & Stock Publishers
199 West 8th Ave., Suite 3
Eugene OR 97401

http://www.wipfandstock.com

Birth Pangs
By Tim Nelson
Copyright©2003, by Tim Nelson
ISBN: 1-59244-368-0
Second Impression

The author can be reached via e-mail:
tim_nelson777@hotmail.com

Thanks to the following people for letting
me borrow their ideas, steal their words:

God, Ryan Carroll, Anthony Cracolice,
Timothy Cracolice, Zebulin Culver,
Gerald Kinneavy, Roger Weaver

and

Wendell Berry, G.K. Chesterton, C.S.
Lewis, Soren Kierkegaard, God.

CONTENTS

PREFACE

Certainly a principal, if not the paramount, death in poetry is that of faith. Though wounded by self-propulsion of Nietzsche's superman, and definitely wobbly from the Enlightenment, she finally succumbed to the ascendancy and primacy of science in our modern version of the West. One can either accept it from me or from W.B. Yeats. To turn to an artist of faith these days is often to turn to a chronicler of cloying truisms or saccharine affirmations of the omniscience and munificence of a god seemingly abandoned a century ago by the intelligensia.

Essentially, without the Yeatsian persistence and breadth of mind to reanimate the dead idea of faith by infusing it with old form and new meaning, the modern artist of faith possesses as much purpose as a Good Humor man in the Sahara-- unless the artist is able to cull from his personal experience illustrations of the necessary tension that mirrors this ultimate frustration, the chasm between the vacuum of modern life and illusory futility of a faith that calls not only for the abnegation of reason, but also the denial of sensual and emotional fulfillment. The artist of faith must forego not Yeats' heavenly mansion, but Coleridge's pleasure dome. He must do so consciously, with the same level of gusto that Nietzsche's Ubermensch embraces the eternal recurrence. It is the struggle to do this that must inform the work of the modern poet of faith.

I believe Tim Nelson captures this truth in this collection. Many of the poems are reflective of the inherent conflict between modern faith and

modern art. Where others may shy away from
personal disclosure and revelations of doubt and
anxiety, Tim speaks with a fresh candor. And Tim
does this without forfeiting variety of style. Some
poems, like "Keeping Out the Rain," are crafted with
a Zen-like sparsity:

It has been said
that one cannot live
in the past. I have
built several houses
there. All are beautiful,
but none keep out the rain.

Others, notably Tim's comic and poignant portrait of
the Eternal City fallen on hard times ("Roma"),
possess a richness of idiom. His influences are as
diverse as his forms; fragments of Yeats, R.S.
Thomas, Carl Sandburg, are easily spotted in the
current of Tim's intellectual stream, down which I
hope you will enjoy your trip.

                    --Anthony Cracolice

To a Young Poet

For the first twenty years you are still growing,
Bodily that is; as a poet, of course,
You are not born yet. It's the next ten
You cut your teeth on to emerge smirking
For your brash courtship of the muse.
You will take seriously those first affairs
With young poems, but no attachments
Formed then but come to shame you,
When love has changed to a grave service
Of a cold queen.

From forty on
You learn from the sharp cuts and jags
Of poems that have come to pieces
In your crude hands how to assemble
With more skill the arbitrary parts
Of ode or sonnet, while time fosters
A new impulse to conceal your wounds
From her and a bold public,
Given to pry.

You are old now
As years reckon, but in that slower
World of the poet you are just coming
To sad manhood, knowing the smile
On her proud face is not for you.

R.S. Thomas

Collected Poems 1945-1990
London: Phoenix Giant, pg. 126.

Double Sorrowed

The marble falls to rubble
before time can meet eternity.
Craftsmen arrive at dawn
to build what is undone.
The king is double sorrowed,
good cannot become great.
What was bound to grow
has suffered in quick death.
The workers turn for home,
the king removes his crown.
The rock crafted back into stone,
he will build alone until undone.

The Harp and the Camera

I do not want a photograph--
sear the image into my mind's eye.

These are not islands with trees on them,
they are the knuckles of a lesser god
who angered the ultimate and was drowned.

The fallen giant's fingers float above the great
expanse. His hands reach out for mercy,
but what is absolute must remain absolute.

I travel across this calmed chaos and ask
myself, "What is required to be alive?"
Green hair grows over the great dead bones
reminding me life demands death.

Do not look at me through a lens,
Breathe and make music through me.

Eve

I cannot say what is
for I am a third rate philosopher
(or so they told me at Oxford).

I shall not speak of what has been
for history is a web fashioned
densely with lies
(or so they taught at the state university).

I will not tell what is to be, for
a false prophet must be put to death
(so I learned in Sunday School);

I know, if she leaves,
it will hurt no more than
removing a single rib.

Neb

Ashes in mouth, ashes in eyes;
the old man thrashed about in
a dead world. Born in his father's
land, but without his mother's tongue.

Raised on shame, Scythian induced,
he circled within the country of his birth.
He rose out of water, was vomited inland,
but clawed his way back north.

Under magnification at university,
his genius only visible to the naked eye.
Snatched by the cloister, forty years
of weeping and gnashing teeth.

At thirty he was born, his tongue loosened
and he bellowed to his mother's father.
Leviathan, he sought an ocean
that had receded into eternity.

The ashes fell: he saw, he spoke,
but who was left to hear his cry?
He let blood for fifty years,
he fell like a spear, like a feather.

Continuous Creation
Newport, Oregon 10/27/01

Spirit breathes spirit
and a child is born.

Each wave is a soul
carried into this garden.

The earth turns, the moon
pulls, the crest grows.

This span from calm to calm
is not chaos, but continuous creation.

It is the womb in
eternity we call time.

The Weight of a Ghost

I am ready to leap at love like faith,
as soon as I see it, but cannot see
faith and my eyes are growing old.

Eighteen years of looking and
scales grow over my eyes. I cannot
deafen the shouts of prophecy; the need
may die, but does not diminish.

What must I do, one who seeks treasure
but is empty-handed? I must stare down
heaven and leap with the weight of a ghost.

6

No Second Cross

The man reaches for a sword
and walks away with a cane.

Did he think he could bend
it into the shape of a heart, or
hammer it into a second cross?

The twig is strong enough for
the fire that must die to be born.

Happiness

I remember the Korean kid,
cheeks chubby from the candy store.
He was happy, he couldn't keep
his teeth behind his lips.

The old man at church, he spoke, and
joy burst from his heart, raced up his
throat, and pushed out his teeth.

I awoke and cried a voiceless
happiness, the voice of tears, the joy
of weeping. My teeth were clenched.

I teared, knowing my brother
happy with nickel candy.
I spoke and heard my
Grandfather yearning for song.

The Heart

And something moves me
to think of her. Maybe, it is
the creation of music. No,
it is the passion of the singer.
I am not sure what he is
saying, but I know that
he believes it.

I dreamt a dream of her,
not grand, but great. Maybe,
it was the port I drank, but
I don't think so. I am
certain it is the thing
we call "the heart."

Faith's Leap

Shame blisters my soul,
promises made, but unkept.
I yearn to be whole,
but fear faith has leapt.
From my injured throat
a dirge, a wassail, a prayer?
I cannot cross the moat,
who will take me there?

The ghost returns,
and lifts the man
who thinks he burns,
across the span
that cannot be measured
by time or bags of
gold, but by the treasure
that hides behind love.

Mortal

A granddaughter is born mortal,
worth the price, if only to be.
The whole of life is the moral,
time is but the blink of eternity.

A grandmother dies, and I am mortal.
Two ticks of the clock, it is me.
The end of the story is the moral,
life is but the breath of eternity.

Roma

It's all tits and ass
in this city of hot, old stone.
A million mopeds taking life for eye,
and El Citta Del Vaticano.

Life is miracle
in this land of constant sun.
In the heart of Christendom,
myocardial infarction.

Exodus from purgatory--
a bus adorned with one crucifix
and one playboy bunny.
Notre Dame, precare enim nostra!

The Shedding of Blood

Who will take the cup,
drink it to its dregs,
and beg "More!"

I know our love
is embodied when we
are in the mouth of the other.

Who will speak with a voice
that truly trembles?
Who will break the crust
of this unpoetic age?

I know her soul
was fleshed for song.
I feel the birth pangs
of a poet.

Where Forest and Plain Meet

The monoliths rise up from underneath
the ancient stands. Florescent greenery
appears on the back of dead flesh:
a great work of divine sorcery.

Will you arise, giant, slumbering elk,
or will the mold overcome you, leaving
no coat of brown? The beast's invasion
of the forest stalls, its slow death slowing.

Human eyes fail to see a picture of love;
In symbiosis the dead and dying live.

Love Is A Squeezed Lemon

I want passion in the form of an A-bomb,
but it dribbles like a squeezed lemon.

I tire of kissing the darkness
when her mouth is in front of mine.

There is a lack of an impression
in the bed where I want her to be.

The words in the book go down easy
with the red of her lips.

I wants to crush mediocrity into zealotry,
but love requires a softer pair of hands.

Virtue

The fire burns,
as unquenchable
as lust or envy.
Some tire of this
simile, but how
long and the naked
hand is still seared?

We continue in fragility
despite our supposed
evolution. We are as
strong as an amoeba,
as intelligent as a fish.

We gained one thing
in our progression--
dissatisfaction.
This virtue makes us
sapient, may we not
be consumed by fire.

Violent Need

A cloud came over
my house yesterday,
and grew dark
with the night.

It is morning, and
I cannot see the sun
through the storm
of my violent need.

The show of strength
that weakens me is
the lightning that hits
both root and trunk.

I yearn for the sun, but
charred roots tether
me to old, secure ground.

Cauldron

Dare she warm her hands
on an unpredictable fire?
The fire keeper can offer
such caution, but passion
proffers no security.

She can choose the cold
dark, and stumble for as
long as her heart beats,
or touch the flame
that will consume her.

Heavy as Mirth

It was not her, but she made me remember:
The beer in our glass darker than the night sky,
our words as heavy as mirth, light as ambrosia.
There was no thought of distance or time.

Three winters and four thousand miles have thawed
since the pint glass overflowed with anything:

My heart is heavy, my mind is light. To a man
lost in a desert, four thousand miles is eternity.

Distance bridged by time.
"Let's have a long pub drink on Friday."
"I do not get in until 10, and even a spry chick like
me will be wiped out."
"Next time, next time is good too."

A Prayer

Let the world that
rushes become still;
Let the voice that
loves say, "I will;"
Let the ocean that
roars be silent;
Let the one who
struggles relent;
Let the drunkard
speak soberly;
Let the cripple
walk gracefully;
Let the demon who
speaks with a sting
be loved by an
angel who can but sing;
Let the writer of
these small words
learn, love is love,
he will be heard.

The Prime Mover Moves

Her core unshakable as
my hate for London.
All have a breaking point:
she is mine. I fear she
cannot be moved and I
am pulled, often against my
will, to her magnanimity.

A word fights and slips
through my lips: "sacrifice."
A foreign and ancient tongue--
the Prime Mover will draw
me away from myself.

God speaks in the voice
of a woman, uttering mysteries
I have long denied. To leave
this hut in the middle of the
woods for the frenzied mass
of thirteen million--

I know I must give all.

Demon Birthed Time

Do not be deceived by the demon-birthed time;
It is no more than a speck on the face of eternity.
These heavy hands that march on, and weigh heavily
upon us, stop for no man, even the sublime.

We often speak of time flying or of being stuck in
quicksand,
but we see with our eyes, this feeble perception.
Nothing is as steady as time until undone,
for it is created being, under another's command.

White

Why do I feel like an
old man watching his
daughter become a bride?

I am neither old nor
father, and you are no
bride, but we grow now
in ways that distance us.

For all that I have taken
and all you would not give,
For tears that would not run
and now will not run dry:

I know I feel old because
I am no longer a boy. And
I see you in white because I
fail to see you any other way.

Mule

She danced our dance with someone else,
and I felt fiery stones in my stomach.
He's doing it wrong, hips not armpits.

I know I am slow and heavy,
but I am as strong as an ox
and tireless as a mule.

Does she have no need
for an old, faithful beast?

24

The World's Unrest

Two things make the world turn:
the naked finger and the burning chest.
Beauty and beauty will not mingle,
and the world can feel no rest.

Red

I look for something red:
blood from a fiery pepper,
a rose as heavy as stone.

I find a man half dead
with the gray of an old leper,
and the weight of being alone.

Weakened

"I would marry you."

"I'm flattered."

"I am not a river
birthed to erode,
I am the rock
that is weakened
grain by grain."

Keeping Out the Rain

It has been said
that one cannot live
in the past. I have
built several houses
there. All are beautiful,
but none keep out the rain.

Open Field

The fruit is bruised because
I chopped down the tree.
The tree stands naked,
I stole its royal clothes.

I awoke in an open field
with all my ribs removed.
I now see everything
for my stole is mystery.

A Sunrise

Above these acres
of green buzz cuts,
beyond this shield
of morning smoke,
hangs a bright orb,
a nuclear orange.

Joy

Joy--just outside the
edge of recollection,
beyond the county line,
out of my jurisdiction.

Illegal

Flagrant kisses explode
and it is not the Fourth of July.
Leftovers from previous years or
purchased prematurely, illegally?

Addiction

I want to write and drink
myself to something,
but my writing has always
been inconsistent and my
drinking even less habitual.

Water

In her presence there is rain.
A touch is the birth of a waterfall.
No desire to cross the ocean,
floating in mystery, that's all.

Well
(thanks to Dave Ried)

He sent her flowers.
Of course, he's sent her flowers many times.
Well, not "of course,"
and not so many times.

Magnanimous

Her strength is her
weakness--tyrannical.
She is dictator. No,
listen, she is prophet.

Rage, sister, rage,
put your heel into my
lazy soul. Burn, burn
for you have divine heat.

Let your weakness be
your strength--magnanimous.
You were born, but
not to peasantry.

Fire

She is fire, I am wood.
She is raging, long I've stood.

August zephyr, blow her heat
through my fingers, down my feet.

Let the fire burn, through my fruit,
she will turn before the root.

Silence

Her breath turns to stone.
Stones too heavy to carry,
too hard to cut. He lacks
skill to fashion them
into armor, magic to turn
them into bread.

"Sweet Lord, purse your lips
and breathe these stones
back to life."

The Sun Shone
(for Carl Sandburg)

You say my world is dark, too dark to see.
I see just fine, I see you.

You need your Southern Cal sunshine to see,
I go blind there.

Give me Olympic Peninsula--so green it's black.
But not for the folks that live there, they see just
fine.

I know Saul saw when blinded on the road to
Damascus.
I know the sun shone the moment Christ died.

Love is Strange Fire
(for Rebecca Joy and Stephen Henry Bonham)

Love is strange fire; it will flicker, but not fail.
One command: stoke the flame, do not hold back.
It is two roads, and to travel is to travail.
No way easy though one leads forward, one back.

Love is a past of wrongs done and life untried,
towers built which are not what they seemed.
It is a future of wrongs undone and self untied,
but bad cannot grow good, it must be redeemed.

Love is two: what we know and what we see.
Man, woman, juxtaposed like body and soul.
The sum, not the parts, of human trinity:
The bond of mind, heart, and the visceral.

What is wholly past becomes Holy
Present; Henry's Joy is Joy's Henry.

No Shame In Dying Old
(Floyd Emanuel Nelson 1911-1998)

She writes, "I hope this letter finds you well and at
peace."
I can only respond, "I wish your hope was full,
for your spilt ink finds me, burdened by the will of
God,
buried by the weight of death, and my empty soul."

It must be made clear--there is no shame in dying old.
When last call is made, drink your dram and go,
new wine will not be poured into old skin, and
grandfathers must die, if young men are to grow.

Threshold

The world moves quickly by on both sides,
and I stand dizzy, but I stand.
I am landlocked by the words of the sages;
I must believe my observance is not in vain.

Stones in one hand, a hole in the other.
Who would believe my burdens
are pleasures, and my wound
smells of the breath of a goddess?

I stand at a threshold I can barely conceive.
The sage in me says,
"Do not open, you will be destroyed."
The fool will not even knock.

Blood

Her fingers reach
beneath my skin
and pierce my vein.

The blood flows,
the written word.

I am weakened from
my sacrifice, angered,
for she is no surgeon,
but a child with a knife
and a careless heart.

Essence

In this dark age,
blind to the image
of God

we stand alone,
far from the throne
of God.

In her essence
is the presence
of God.

45 Degrees

The wind pushes the grass
to a 45 degree angle, not less.

The sun must be inspired
to make winter appear retired.

Will we live in perpetual Spring
or is Winter only bluffing?

She tosses my hair, the wind. Her
aspiration is a long, wet winter.

Waiting to be Born

Is there music in the words I write?
for there is none in the keys I strike
nor the strings I scratch. Is there
grace in the movement of this pen?
for my body only stumbles and falls.
Is there any love in me? for all I feel
is the death of rage and the coma of despair.

My mind only brings barricades,
and the desires of my heart, death.
I have long since lost the strength
to persevere, and yet, I am beckoned,
pushed, carried, to a future I have not
imagined, an embrace I have yet
to feel.

The Juaquin Valley

He drives into the wasteland,
his thoughts verdant with her.
The wind embraces, sardonic friend,
the sun an eternal cinder.

The rain does not fall, and
the snow has long since thawed.
He carries on into the wasteland,
with himself, and his thought.

Earth in Opposition

The earthly opposites pull,
tear, and make whole.

Solitude, a gift known to heal,
but never to wholeness.

One must drop his weapon,
raising arms sword less.

Lions will tear limb from limb,
God, as woman, will reassemble.

The Half Truth of Night
(thanks to Ella Taylor)

The self is labyrinth, the map is found
in wisdom, and her sister, folly.
The keepers of this beautiful bonfire
beckon all into the sacred sorority.

Tragedy torn from the life of dust--
silence falls on quiet already still.
As we search, we are searched,
all we determine is not our will.

We learned, to be sinful is to understand,
to die old is to learn much madness,
and to live without dying is the same as death.

The tryst is the half we understand,
thoughts of destination our madness,
and the half truth of night, death.

Reach

Reach--dig, if you must,
into this thing called soul.
If nothing else, shake it
like an empty toner cartridge.
It must be good for one more job.

If not, remove it.
Graft in a new one,
like skin, no matter the cost.

An Admission
(for Jeanette Winterson)

You touch me in the one place
I believe I must hide.
I do not fear being destroyed;
I am vanquished by the thought
of being left undone.

I pray that one will remove
my ugliness, piece by jagged
piece, until I am nothing, and
then reassemble me, pure.

A Basket of Stones and Flowers

If my petition were too broad
I would pull it off her shoulders,
but I know her strength
for each day she carries a
basket of stones and flowers.
Despite the load, each grimace
is washed as she climbs
to something I cannot see.

I love her, and though I
cannot turn her stones to bread,
I will carry them. I love her,
and though I cannot make
her flowers grow, I will point
them towards the sun.

Iron Sharpens Iron

Iron sharpens iron,
pierces the savior's side.

Insult upon insult,
a thief is crucified.

Stone stacked on stone, old hate
sparks a fire, burns a saint.

We must die before death,
grow weary and not faint.

My Heart is Held Captive

My heart is held captive, and I can neither
leave nor fully love until I am released.
I was fettered without my knowing,
but I have stayed willingly.
Now I must make her heart my home
or find a new abode.

Open your ears, open your heart
for my breath will be mumbled
through tears of salt and blood.

Pull me down for my hands are nailed.
Or push the spear swiftly through,
for I cannot love if I cannot love you.

Poems

Poems are large rocks,
yet to be hewn, and
put into a wall.

Poems are virgins,
beautiful because of
what they may become.

Poems are rough agate,
only gravel until
they are polished.

A Plea

Look at my brazen face,
is it not sweet?
Touch my face,
feel my heart's heat
burning your hand
and fueling your soul.

Your eyes unshackle my
heart and throw down
the barriers in my mind;
Your lipstick's red pulls
the blood through my
hardened veins.

Don't tell me about "his way."
Damn his eyes: see your
future in mine. Damn his kiss,
his smile, his thoughts.

A History

The discovery of gun powder-
each year Americans shout
praise into the summer sky.

To pack black powder--
a mountain torn asunder,
its secrets, secret no more.

One placed iron on wood--
an act of dark foreboding,
many have fallen, many will.

The Words

The words do not come
like water from a spring.
They are in the rocks
and must be mined.

I have only a pick and
these arms--both weary
and bound soon to break.

Words dug up are not
platinum or silver,
maybe tin or copper,
but mostly fool's gold.

A poet is an unhappy being whose heart is torn by secret sufferings, but whose lips are so strangely formed that when the sighs and cries escape them, they sound like beautiful music.

Soren Kierkegaard

Either/Or
Princeton, NJ: Princeton University Press, pg. 19.

Thinking and Thought, Writing and Word

The greatness of the poet can be measured by the depth of his eyes (Do not confuse depth for physical sight, Homer and Milton were our greatest seers).

Give me a poet who has not sabotaged his life and I will give you an exception.

Word is the hammer, silence is the anvil.

The poet is the poem and his words are dross.

A society that silences its poets and prophets should not complain about the dullness of life.

To write is to steal.

A man writes because he will not cry; a woman writes because she will not scream.

Does the artist see truths that are not there or are scientists indignant because they do not see truth as well as artists?

There are some sentiments that words cannot express. No, this is the job of the poets.

The pen and the scalpel both heal and hurt.

The muse is stronger than the man.

We eagerly embrace the melancholic artist when he creates things we like, but when he does not, he is sick and needs help.

Many have relegated the sublime to the artist, but I have seen a man with a 5th grade education build a house that made me dream of heaven.

Why is it so strange to us that God would be concerned about the finiteness of his creation? It is only man who carelessly destroys what he creates.

Spontaneity in art is false, we want it to be easy.

Every thing is measured by its degree of difficulty.

It does not matter what a man can do, but what he actually does.

Adventure is a new book in an old house.

Passion is more important than ability for passion guarantees what even genius cannot.

Thinking is action, and yet, it should precede some other action.

One's expectations cannot be too high, but they can be wrong.

One must believe that he will know because he cannot know that he will believe.

Truth makes fools of us all.

All one needs to know he does not yet know.

The last question to be answered, if at all, is why.

Human logic may be redundant.

Rebuke from a friend is better than compliment from an enemy.

The world is flat, what goes around does not always come around.

For virtue there must be censorship: if we are to herald good, we must condemn evil.

The only way to enjoy what is temporary is not to be dependent on it.

In a fast world one must learn to be slow.

It takes a wise man to listen to one he does not trust.

Go easy on a child and he will prove himself difficult.

The fool attempts to understand what he already enjoys.

Having done no wrong, if a person apologizes, she feels offended.

The only way to measure an activity is with a goal. The only real goal is the ideal.

He who is content with good works may forsake great works.

Wisdom is power, knowledge is raw material.

The desert is no wasteland, for not a drop of water is wasted.

Suffering

Suffering does not produce virtue, it reveals one's character.

There is no short road to fervor, a nation, community or individual, must go through the place of suffering.

To arrive at the city of humility, one must traverse the mire of humiliation.

Healing is the ends and means, there is no wholeness here.

Not all who hurt were victimized, some were born to suffer.

The university of old, and the cloister, expected excellence from each man that entered, even at the price of destroying him. The modern university has one requirement: money. The modern seminary has no requirements.

Pain remembers, pleasure forgets.

It is strange to enjoy pain, but thoroughly human to enjoy the memory of pain.

Sorrow can be felt by a single individual, but for joy, two or more must be present.

No matter how good a lot a man is given, he desires suffering.

No man suffers silently who suffers truly.

Happiness is fleeting, suffering lasts a lifetime.

What is suffering but the attempt to rectify what no human being can?

Some will suffer much because some refuse to suffer at all.

We do not enjoy pleasure to cope with suffering; we suffer to prepare for pleasure.

Do not pour warm water on frostbite: do not sing a happy song to a sad man.

One who thinks much is not happy often.

Optimism is a poor substitute for happiness.

If we were happy, we would not desire heaven.

All have lived in sorrow, some call it happiness, some call it sorrow.

Desire=not satisfied.

The most terrible balance is holiness and love.

Bitterness is anger that has been kept alive only to rot.

Some anger is bred merely for the sensation.

The "why" question, if committed, leads only to bitterness.

He who does not embrace solitude will never know himself.

Do not tell a man to be patient, do not encourage him to be spontaneous, let him find his own way to consistency.

God and Theology

All desire is a desire to be God.

For faith there must be the possibility of despair.

It is not blind faith to look while you jump.

What is "soul" but our attempt to throw a word at what we do not understand?

What is chance but man's admission that he does not know and is not in control?

Our soul is a harlot and a Trinitarian: she dances with heart, mind and loins.

That one's strength can be one's weakness is fact; that one's weakness can be one's strength is miracle.

We prove God when we laugh.

We have kings because we want to see God.

Fate exists only in the mind of one who has no faith.

The only way to remedy guilt is to admit wrong.

Love is not God.

Even what we know is mysterious. For we do not know why or how we know.

One can be in bondage to his desires but unless he has desire he cannot be free.

66

If one cannot afford to succumb, how can he afford to be tempted?

If one cannot afford to be tempted, he is already in hell.

Heaven and hell are everywhere for they dwell in the heart of man.

Do not ask to know what the mind cannot contain or we may fall further than Adam.

The first mistake is to believe we understand already. The second mistake is to believe we are not compelled to understand.

Absolute freedom is no freedom at all.

All anger is ultimately directed towards God.

It is not a question of whether or not one loses his innocence, but how and what she replaces it with.

Atheism is the great temper-tantrum.

Christianity is difficult because faith is difficult.

To doubt is only to question, to despair is to be unsatisfied with God.

Know yourself by loving your neighbor.

To kill one's neighbor is instinctual, to love him is not.

Teach me humility and become a saint.

"Magic" only means that we do not know why a certain thing works.

Memory is the grand tool of salvation.

Truth may be ugly, but ugliness is not truth.

We may receive blessing because of failure, but failure is no blessing.

Ignorance is not faith, but the ignorant can be faithful.

If virtue cannot be taught, it cannot be learned.

The difference between commitment and intellectual ascent is the difference between heaven and hell. (Thanks to RC)

Salvation by Grace Alone is like a man so enamored by his legs he does not walk anywhere. (Thanks to ZB)

Earth is both heaven and hell, this is purgatory.

There is no returning to Eden: Heaven is a city.

Heaven is pure hope, hell is despair itself.

If all is one, there can be no love.

The zenith of religion is hope: I am content, but I want something more.

To be righteous is to see sin in one's life and to make every attempt to remove it. But when he sees sin in another, the righteous man must resist the temptation

68

to root it out.

The only easy way to combat sin is with another sin.

One should not confuse what she wants to do with what she should do, but to do so is human.

Salvation is escaping with one's life.

What is original sin, but to betray the one we ought to love?

Faith means not knowing, yet knowing,

Existence is a battle, and the human soul is the battlefield.

We believe before we know.

Individuals who do not believe in God will play God.

The true offense of Christianity is that it denies my divinity.

We do not get what we want because we are not who we think we are.

No one walks away from life unscathed.

To reduce the role of faith is to misuse it.

We are told that the following will not enter the kingdom of heaven: sexual immorality, impurity, debauchery, idolatry, witchcraft, hatred, jealousy, rage, selfish ambition, dissensions, factions, envy, drunkenness orgies etc. It must be asked if these are the things that prevent a person from entering the kingdom or are they signs of the thing that prevents entrance.

If we do the right thing long enough we may desire righteousness.

If one is going to be discontent he should make it look like desire.

The human trinity consists of heart, mind and soul.

Why are we here? To learn what we are not.

Be still and know that you are not God.

When the rich man dies he leaves behind the same thing the poor man does--everything.

Emotions (excluding love) and Dispositions

When one gives up ignorance, he must also give up security.

Money provides the illusion of security.

It is easy to confuse sympathy for affection.

If feeling good makes it right, how good must one feel?

Hesitation is only good if it is perceived as patience.

Ambition is like humility, if it must be announced, it is not present.

What is conscience but the presence of God? Who would go against his strongest desire?

There is no greater sin than ennui.

Sometimes when we say something is right we only mean that it makes us feel comfortable.

Envy is a negative commodity. The more one desires of others the less he has.

Sometimes the right thing feels wrong--do it anyway.

No matter how hard one tries, he cannot divorce his character from his actions.

It is a long road from the self.

We can run away from everything but ourselves.

Empathy--the one thing we expect when we speak.

Living on regrets makes for long nights and limited days.

Will power is an amazing thing, it is an amazingly inconsistent thing.

We are masters of our emotions and mastered by our emotions.

Self-pity is partially concealed anger.

Being social is not frightening. Neither is being alone; it is the transition between the two that causes fear.

Reason well, but remember to think at all causes pain.

Need is the greatest word.

Respected is the adult word for cool.

Flattery must be specific and positive or it is insult.

If one confuses guilt and shame, he will never be free.

"Tortured genius" is redundant.

Genius is too heavy to bear, it must be breathed.

Do not confuse genius and intelligence, they may not overlap.

There is no purely intellectual genius; a genius is revealed by his body of work.

All geniuses appear deranged, for their thinking is utterly new.

We are not offended by arrogance, but by arrogance punctuated with humility.

We live in a society that readily accepts arrogance, if and only if, it is accompanied by excellence.

The Elitists: all educated people who do not accept the speaker's point. The Ignorant: all others who disagree.

To be aware of our own thoughts is the first step towards vanity, madness and despair, but it is also the first step towards wisdom.

Coming to terms with one's feelings is the same as getting over them.

We can never mete out justice to ourselves.

No matter how great or poor a power, ours is the most difficult to quantify.

The Prime Mover is fear.

Some fears must be overcome, others circumvented. The individual is forced to choose.

Fear is always present where faith is absent.

There is no fear of what one does not care about.

To have no desire is not to fear.

We fear because we are not the center of the universe.

It is easy to be fearful, difficult to be courageous. And yet, fear is the prerequisite for courage.

The blind man must still look at himself.

Now that I see I cannot not see.

Relations and Institutions

The problem with overly conservative institutions (if by conservative we mean cautious) is that they often become anti-intellectual.

A country does not have a soul, it possesses the mob.

If there is no trust between peoples there can be no morality.

We are all normal because we have all sinned.

Science makes itself to be, if not the only authority, the final authority. In doing so, it makes a mockery of itself.

We have laws to protect the body, but our minds are free to abuse.

He who distrusts authority the most, doubts himself the least.

A sports fan is more likely to be a patriot; for he sees himself as part of the team.

Other people's losses are incidental.

The loser remembers the battle longer.

Where two or three are gathered there is either honesty or hospitality, and these two separate kinds of pain.

Modern science is fueled faithlessness.

Life fully lived is never fully private.

Every man is every man for he believes he is not.

A big union functions the same as a big corporation.

Education is no guarantee against foolishness.

Nature is not our enemy though we are often hers.

All relationships are pathological.

One's hometown is much like a lover--when distant she is sorely missed and fiercely loved. When present, she bores and is likely to blackmail.

Something that is safe for all is useless for all.

Your hometown is your mother, she is not for you.

Every organization needs a man who will deliberately rock the boat, think outside the box, imitate the Baptist, is wild.

The Church and the Russian Army are the only institutions that shoot their wounded.

The Church may be a hospital, but it is not a retirement center.

No road is too rough if there are friends at the end of it.

Time

Aging now, but immortal once.

Human beings created time; for eternal beings have no need for it.

My heart is the measure of time.

We think in time and assume that God does too.

When time ends?

Both the past and the future are judged by the present.

Even hindsight can be fantastical.

Call a thing immortal and it will die.

There is no final exit.

Eternal life?

It is all history--the present and future do not exist.

Live posthumously, but do not posthumously live.

Time is Eternity fallen.

Time is the curse.

Near Allied to Humor

A flautist may be many things, but he is never intimidating.

He who straddles the fence will eventually crush his testicles.

One can systematize his sock drawer, but he should not do the same to God.

Can we count the breaths of a man? Yes, once he is dead.

If arrogance put you underground, arrogance will not resurrect you.

When sad, write. When happy, continue doing whatever brings happiness.

Do not shout at a deaf man, he can see you just fine.

"Silence is golden" does not mean that silence has the value of gold, but that it is expected of the aged.

I sometimes make the same mistake twice. It is usually more times that that.

Never trust a man who claims to be both intelligent and handsome.

A essay without errors is an essay that has not been read.

Fuel for fire is good, but only if one plans to burn something.

78

Even the solipsist wishes to be heard.

The one thing a strong man cannot bear is his own strength.

I prefer to do my dancing vicariously.

Beware of the man who calls for unity the loudest, he wants to be your king.

Be tactful even in private for someone always hears.

Beware of preaching that is emotional but not emotive.

"If you wish to know a man you must walk in his shoes." "I am a thief, I have walked in many men's shoes."

Obese people talk a lot about "the inside." Adonises talk a lot about themselves.

Spirituality without religion is like breath without blood (it only occurs in lower life forms).

Growing old beats the alternative.

For the typical grandfather, everything is too quiet except his grandson's rock 'n' roll.

The fool is rarely also coward.

To belabor a point, it must have already been made.

No list is exhaustive though many are exhausting.

An Environmentalist: one who wishes to love things that cannot hurt her.

I will speak the truth, and when I do not know the truth, I will defend my friends.

What do the content write? A shopping list.

Child: "What is a theologian?"
Father: "Someone who makes God disappear."

Eventually the rubber will hit the road, and I hope I have both hands on the steering wheel.

If one cannot be the sexiest at least she can be sexist.

Joseph Campbell tells us to follow our bliss, but what if she says "No"?

I want the vanities of life, but I do not want to be vain.

If this is sobriety, no wonder people get drunk.

If a certain individual says that a certain rock 'n' roll band will save rock 'n' roll she understands neither salvation nor rock 'n' roll.

Welcome to the wasteland called manhood, you are one of many winners.

Patience involves more waiting than I would have hoped for.

A syllogism is dangerous; dangerous is a syllogism.

Do not ask a question just to hear yourself talk.

80

I am ready for a devolution.

It is as if we are blind to the good we receive and bionic to everything else.

What does not kill me now may kill me later.

A child who loves her parents the least is the first to show up when they die.

If you wish to get someone off your back, be overly happy.

The guilty always speak first.

Present day teetotalism is a product of one of two things: alcoholism is near or one is hung over from the prohibition.

I am an adult now and I am not impressed (with adulthood or myself).

Be leery of a man who wishes to be a leader, but do not kill him.

Beware the man who only opens his mouth to switch feet.

One can only tell so much from one who has a nice voice: the speaker has a nice voice.

A parachute only works because it is kept closed by many cords.

Is the glass half full or half empty? It depends on how thirsty you are.

Sometimes I fear that I am a man trapped inside a man's body.

Sharing is a great idea when one wants what another has.

If a man presents himself without need, he will never have a wife.

I am not in a hurry for love, but I wish it was in a hurry for me.

If a man cannot satisfy one woman he should not acquire a harem.

Romantic love is madness, but all wish to be mad.

No one chooses to marry a fool, but many find themselves married to one.

No man is as big as a baby.

One may fall off a building or into cow shit, but she cannot fall into love.

When a woman is persistent in her demonstration of affection for a man we are told that it is love and the man owes her an opportunity. When a man acts in the same manner it is called stalking and he can go to jail.

Ugly women are the cause for much mourning.
Beautiful women more so.

If a man marries an ugly woman he will not be married long.

82

Death, Suicide and Madness

What is madness, but any language not readily understood by the masses?

In a mad world is it healthier to be insane?

We love the quick answer so much that we are quick to consider suicide and apocalypse which are not ends or answers.

The insane man has not lost his mind, but his history.

To kill oneself is to bequeath a curse to one's loved ones. Suicide cures depression like sex cures STDs.

Alcoholism is the coward's suicide (or a desperate attempt to live).

Death becomes us all, it is the one thing we agree on.

Mathematicians often go mad because mathematics is near allied to madness.

Death is not staring mortality in the face, but the person of God.

It is not thinking that drives one to insanity, but insisting that the world always to be logical.

Narcissism: "I think therefore, I am."

One must die to live. The suicide will not do this, it is the one thing he will not do.

Every individual must die, but the suicide kills everyone but himself.

Suicide is an individual's last effort to be in control of death.

To commit suicide is to enter the lowest realm of narcissism.

The suicide refuses to recognize any will but his own.

Narcissism exists because the self is too small a world for the self.

One who is addicted is enthralled with what enslaves him.

If I said that I had hit my breaking point would you think I had become successful in my chosen profession or that I had an emotional breakdown?

To make a brainwashed mind healthier, poison it.

Academia--a place half way between depression and death.

The price of life is life.

Voices? My own voice is deafening.

To be a poet one must die.

We do not fear death, we fear death's consistency.

If a life is not worth living it is not worth taking.

The answer for depression is manual labor.

84

Dialogue

There is no leap to faith, faith is the leap.

How can John Calvin be forgiven?

If the Pope is the anti-Christ so is Martin Luther.

Eliot is right to recognize that Christianity is communal before it is individual, but Kierkegaard speaks to the deeper angst.

If Thoreau's writings are untrustworthy because he took his clothes home to wash them, and Wendell Berry is to be discounted because he made a living as a full-time professor, we are all charlatans.

In pantheism everything is God. In Calvinism, everything is God's will. In both, there is no true distinction between transcendence and immanence.

The German language was meant to be heard above the roar of the factory, amidst the din of gunfire.

Of course Luther started a rebellion. The question is should he have started a rebellion.

No one comes to know the Lord through his intellect, God is a subject.

Scriptural error? The problem is human.

Remember not to anthropomorphize animals, one needs a soul to experience pleasure.

To argue for predestination is to assume complete

85

knowledge of God's nature.

Delight yourself in the Lord and he will change your desires.

The Calvinist must ask himself-- "Is my faith strong enough to accept hell?"

It is enough to believe that God is sovereign, to seek how is to limit Him.

Sin may be inevitable, but it is never permissible.

There are only two moral judgments: what is good and how does one obtain it?

Internal truth is more important than external error.

Intellect without empathy is worthless.

Those who study history are still doomed to repeat it.

What changes us most is prayer during adversity.

In one respect we are all early Christians for all people of faith start at the same place. On the other hand, we have tradition.

Ethics requires the transcendent: "Be perfect as I am perfect."

The Greek man says, "I have a body, I have a soul." But what is it that does the possessing?

How can predestination be seen as anything other than fate, which is purely pagan?

86

Predestination is the absent watch maker: Calvin is a deist.

If one wishes to reform, he should not mistake chopping for pruning.

All theology is a theology of suffering.

The true absurdity of the incarnation is that it was not I.

Kierkegaard was the enemy of pretense.

The modern minister is a little less than the modern politician.

Some things must be stolen if they are to be possessed at all.

Underneath every evil is perverted good.

What was the incarnation but a sneak attack?

History is a controlled riot.

The law is slow, but the fist is fast.

A sinless God who makes others sin is a mad god.

Where the intelligent gather geniuses steal.

Better to read the wrong books than none at all.
Better still to read the right books and get the wrong answers.

The Marxist will do anything to eradicate poverty but

love the poor person.

To say that it takes a village to raise a child is a moot point for every child is raised in some kind of community.

Poets write on ideal love not because it is prevalent but because it is possible.

My belief is clear until I must explain it to another.

Gravity always pulls us down, we must take ourselves lightly if we hope to fly.

To say that we always chose our greatest desire is a tautology, but even this does not get us anywhere.

If Luther was a corrective for the Roman Church, Kierkegaard was a corrective for Luther and Calvin.

Bono has not out sung his voice, he has forsaken his passion.

I am tired of individuals who decry the infallibility of the pope, but have never thought to question themselves.

The Reformation abolished the Church.

True humility gets one a cross.

A man is old when his regrets overshadow his dreams.

It is not that it is more difficult to be a saint in the city, it is difficult to be a saint anywhere.

If the study of theology does not produce humility, it is failure.

Spong chips away at the pedestal he stands on.

One does not go crazy by thinking, but by thinking the thought that stops thought.

It is not what is similar between two things that draws a man's attention, but what sticks out.

The fan and the patriot are both a part of the mob.

How can faith alone be the prescription for salvation if we are told that demons believe?

Neither faith nor works should be seen as the cause for our salvation--they are co-determinous.

If God wants all to be saved (i.e. "the world") but predetermines some for damnation, we have a senile or capricious God.

Even if the doctrine of predestination were true, it fails to teach one how to live.

The early call to existentialism was not a call to leave the Church.

If one takes God from Kierkegaard, she is left with a void.

Molin's God is ultimately, the counter-factuals of freedom.

There is no "elusive common core" unless we are willing to talk about sin.

For God to be sovereign, the individual must be able to disobey him, thwart his will.

If man does not have something he would die for he is not yet alive.

If we are totally depraved, there is no value in any argument.

Women, Sex, Love and Beauty

There are a million miles between the mind and heart.

Are the desire to marry and the desire to desire marriage reconcilable?

I do not fear commitment, it is the decision to commit that makes me tremble.

Men promise practice, women the possibility of intimacy.

To be romantic one must continue to want what he already has.

Love is not blind, it only sees what is there. Hate is blind.

We are told that wanting is better than having, but only because having is closer to losing.

Desire for woman is like a storm, it will pass (and it will come again).

When a girl smiles the day brightens. When a woman smiles the world is on fire.

In or out of love, we expect too much of it.

Love is like a summer day (winter is coming, but so is spring).

There is no viable connection between marriage and dating, it is like the man who raised himself half way back from the dead.

Men are insane and women are incompetent
psychiatrists.

On a frost bitten limb one should pour cold water not
warm. The same is true for the heart.

Real romance must include fear.

A man who is vulnerable may be seen as "high-
maintenance" and/or a "mamma's boy."

What is desire but cloaked need?

Sex was created for marriage not marriage for sex.

Pleasure's trinity: me, here, now.

Pleasure points to what it cannot offer.

Be leery of a woman whose sexuality speaks louder
than her personhood. Avoid the woman whose
sexuality is her personhood.

When a woman accuses a man of being immature she
often only means that he does not act like a woman.

Women encourage men to cry by crying, but men
only feel free to cry when women refrain.

Princesses should not complain that there are so few
kings when they will not be queens.

He who finds a way to harden his heart will find a
way to the brothel.

A woman is more likely to act like a concubine when treated like a princess than a queen.

Love works if we work at love for love always works.

The only way to forego suffering is to forsake love.

The one who scorns his lover creates the perfect muse.

Let's dig away the sediment and get down to the bedrock of love.

A man wishes to lust and a woman wishes to be lusted after.

Flattery is not love.

Love is duty, but duty is not love.

Love is a lout.

Love is a lazy prodigy.

If a man becomes what a woman makes him, he will no longer be attractive to women.

Modern American culture is emasculated and has the nerve to ask "Where are all the men."

Expectations should not amass higher than forgiveness.

Happiness in marriage cannot be a goal, it must be a by-product.

Spouses must be students of each other.
To grab at intimacy produces alienation.

Divorce is the ultimate rejection.

The hardest thing on a marriage is self-pity.

The removal of Adam's rib foreshadowed the
removal of Adam and Eve from the garden.

God created a helpmate because Adam needed help.

Sometimes the helper knows more than the one she
helps.

Listen my son, if you do not wish to ravish her, do
not kiss her.

Do not oral sex and cannibalism have the same root
desire?

Romance novels are pornography's equivalent.

Hate is the emotion most similar to love.

Romance is the missing rib.

Man: She who desires me is suspect.
Woman: I want to be the center of his universe, but
if he makes me so I will resent it.

In love, we should not confuse duty with pride.

Deluded women seek men with money; deluded men
seek women and money.

Double seduction is sour, unless it is perfect.

94

The man who will not commit asks for the undeniable.

Yes, I have a strange understanding of romance, it includes me.

Love is sadness.

What does love require? Oneself.

Man desires woman and woman yearns to be desired by man.

Women wish to marry bad boys and make them good, men hope to marry perfect girls who will stay perfect.

There are only three headings for sexuality: celibacy, monogamy and other.

Celibacy and monogamy are both sacrifices, but the former is chosen less frequently.

Marrying into money may be incidental, but it is never accidental.

Let none say that love cannot embolden belief, let none say there can be belief without love.

Sex is not a balm for past hurts, we heal the hurt by resuffering it.

For some, the willingness to love is the test. For some, accepting love is the only test.

One jumps to the conclusion of celibacy, but the waiting is in the doing and not doing.

The waiting is often the means and end.

A sexual addiction is an unwillingness to love, and more importantly, an unwillingness to be loved.

It is better to marry than burn, but only if one knows marriage will stop the burning.

To commit one must chose to forget.

A challenge for any man is to lust for what he cannot see.

Love is more confusing than death because it is avoidable.

The majority of people marry due to loneliness or lust.

A man who wishes to have dominion over his sexual energies, at any price, should groom bitterness.

Love's only guarantee is death.

Romantic games do not make love more fun, but more meaningful.

It is the bravery of women that makes love possible.

The homosexual man desires a righteous man. So does the homosexual woman.

There is no such thing as equality, and secretly, we all prefer this.

Feminism has failed whenever women simply imitated men.

Sexism is a great insecurity in relation to the other sex.

Those who refrain from love do so because love is difficult.

One must be independent before he can be truly dependent.

In the end, women want money. From the beginning, men need body.

When women lead, men get in the way.

To be modern is to be unbeautiful.

The problem with beauty is that one is quick to confuse it with God.

Both men and women are obsessed with beauty-- women with the becoming and staying, men with obtaining and keeping.

Beauty is masochistic--this constant cycle of hurting and healing.

Be extremely leery of Theology that is not beautiful.

Beauty is obnoxious when present, even more so when absent.

Every man, when young, learns not to stare into the face of beauty.